AN
UNNATURAL HISTORY
OF
DEATH VALLEY

WITH REFLECTIONS ON
THE VALLEY'S VARMINTS, VIRGINS,
VANDALS AND VISIONARIES

by
Paul Bailey

Illustrations by Bill Bender

Library of Congress Cataloging in Publication Data
Bailey, Paul Dayton, 1906-
        An unnatural history of Death Valley.

        1. Death Valley—History—Addresses, essays, lectures.
2. Bailey, Paul Dayton, 1906- —Addresses, essays,
lectures. I. Death Valley, '49ers. II. Title.
F868.D2B27   979.4'87   78-21578
ISBN 0-912494-30-1
ISBN 0-912494-31-X pbk.

Published by
Chalfant Press, Inc.
450 East Line Street
Bishop, CA 93514

For
Death Valley '49ers, Inc.
Death Valley, CA 92328

Book design: Russ Johnson

AN UNNATURAL HISTORY OF DEATH VALLEY

Photographs Courtesy of:
  Death Valley National Monument
  CHP Officer Dave Steuber
  Dist. Att. Buck Gibbons

  Paul Bailey, George and Ann Pipkin, George Koenig and
  Russ and Ann Johnson Collections

To all of the Death Valley '49ers —
both the pioneers and those of
recent vintage, and to
Evelyn.

Contents

Paul Bailey.

PAUL BAILEY

An introduction, by Walt Wheelock

Paul Bailey was born almost "three score and ten years ago" in the small Mormon village of American Fork. This town was founded in 1850 in the then State of Deseret. Maps of the western United States of that period show that the Mormon settlements were located in what was then known as The Great American Desert; so Paul from the very time of his conception was a product of our desert regions.

But at first, he little realized that he was living in a desert, for the Latter Day Saints had transformed this area into what Paul described as, "The Utah Valley of my youth was a land of pristine beauty . . . This valley, some thirty miles south of Salt Lake City, has a sweep and grandeur comparable to anything Switzerland has to offer."* But away from the bottom lands the slopes were covered with greasewood, fragrant Mormon tea and late-blooming rabbit brush with its masses of yellow blooms, all desert flora.

Here Paul spent his early youth, studying in the public schools and attempting to avoid the after-school Saints' classes. While his ancestors on both sides had been devout Saints (he tells that both of his grandfathers first met in the Territorial Penitentiary where they were each serving time for the infamous crime of Mormon polygamous cohabitation), Paul's father, Eli, tended to backslide, enjoying a cigarette, failing to attend all of the numerous church-oriented meetings—in fact, seeming to have a mind of his own.

The Church had been, even from the times of Brigham Young, actively engaged in activities that would bring in monies

---

From a talk delivered by Paul Bailey at the Author's Breakfast, 27th Annual Encampment of Death Valley '49ers, Death Valley, California, November 1976.

Death Valley '49ers, Hugh Tolford and Paul Bailey.

from the gentiles to support the Saints' culture. Even in the Gold Rush days, Salt Lake City did a brisk trade, selling beer and whiskey, at whatever the tariff would bear, to the passing Forty-niners. Shortly after the turn of the century, it was believed that if sugar mills were to be constructed, the raising of sugar beets would be profitable. Paul writes, "The Utah-Idaho Sugar Company, owned and dominated by the Mormon Church, saw fit to promote Eli Bailey in spite of his cigarettes and laxity in tithing... a new and modern factory was to be built at Grants Pass (Oregon). Eli was tendered an all-important foremanship on this wonderful new project."

So the Baileys moved on to Oregon, but as happened with all of Eli's hopes and dreams, this one failed. The non-Mormon farmers of Oregon were not charmed with the possibility of growing a new crop and the project was abandoned.

It was decided to move the factory to eastern Washington to the small town of Toppenish. Eli was again selected to supervise the construction. And so again the Bailey family was to move to the semi-arid Great Basin Desert in the Yakima Valley. Again luck was not with Eli and poverty held the Baileys in its grip. Furthermore, his parents' life was strained by the combination of the marginal economy and the ever-increasing rift between a devout mother and a Jack-Mormon father. It was too much for Paul and he fled back to American Fork, where he lived until he reached early manhood. (For a more complete saga of Bailey in Utah read his book *Polygamy Was Better Than Monotony.*)

In order to put himself through college, Paul went to work as an orderly in the County Hospital in Salt Lake City. He hated every moment of this, but it had its compensations, for on the same grounds was the Nurses' Home, where also lived the student nurses, of which "twice a year came in a crop from the Utah towns, who were a sight for any lonely young man to see. "My gaze con-

15

Author, publisher, historian, raconteur Paul Bailey at the Author's breakfast during the Death Valley '49er Encampment.

stantly and covetously followed the untouchables through their nurse-training on the wards of the County Hospital."

But Paul was never one to be completely frustrated, and he found that despite the rules and regulations, perhaps he just might be able to touch one, the most beautiful Evelyn Robison from Fillmore. But there was little more than a mere touch, as Evelyn was stricken with an illness, which forced her to drop out of training and return to Fillmore.

Three years passed and both were now far from Utah. Evelyn was again in training, now at the Los Angeles General Hospital and Paul was scratching for a fingerhold in newspapering and sustaining himself at a typographical plant in Los Angeles. They were wed in the Church's Mission Home in Los Angeles at Christmas time in 1927 and together entered into what was to become a new life in the fields of newspapers, writing and publishing, where he was to gain nationwide fame.

It was also in that year that Paul and Evelyn first visited Death Valley. Driving over primitive roads, through deep dust and sand, they made their way with water canteens and camping gear lashed to the running boards of their small car. For the next fifty years they have continued to return to the so-called Valley of Death, both on their own and with the Fortyniners.

Evelyn and Paul were in attendance at the Centennial Gathering of 1949, although they had come with a group from E Clampus Vitus. Paul and the other Clampers set up at Cow Camp on an overlooking mesa, while Evelyn spent her time with the other gals in the nearby Widows' Camp. The next morning they attempted to reach the shindig in Desolation Canyon in that wild melee, but Paul tells that in delightful detail in the opening chapter, "Biggest Birthday Bust."

In the meantime, back in Los Angeles, he worked as a typesetter for the *Examiner* and the *Herald,* while struggling with the

17

hope of somehow becoming a writer. After-hours he beat out copy and before too long was being published in small magazines, historical quarterlies and newspaper supplements. But he had not neglected his printing activities and became well-known in the field of creative typography, serving in a supervisory capacity for Homer Boelter, who ran probably the outstanding "fine press" in Southern California, rivaling the work of the Grabhorns and Nash in the San Francisco Bay area. But he always looked forward to a career as an author. He was successful in creating fine novels based on Mormon subjects, including *For This My Glory,* a story of the *jornada* of the Mormon Battalion as they struggled across the Imperial Valley desert toward Los Angeles.

Trying for a while, but not too successfully to earn a living as a reporter, he suddenly found himself back in the printing trade, now as the owner, publisher and editor for the *Eagle Rock Advertiser.* Here with long killing hours, both for himself and for Evelyn, they managed to pull a failing neighborhood advertising sheet into a successful newspaper. Unfortunately along came World War II, and the War Production Board held such neighborhood "rags" in low esteem—allotting them little newsprint. In order to keep alive, ads were sharply cut to provide room for story material and revenues dropped. To survive, Paul took over the editorship of an in-house organ, the *Lockheed Star,* and in his spare time returned to writing, producing his definitive *Jacob Hamblin, Buckskin Apostle,* the first of a long series he produced (and is still producing) in this genre.

Going back to the War Production Board, he found that paper was readily available for book publishing, and so was born *Westernlore Press,* which has become one of the outstanding publishers of Western Americana. Not only are the Press' works well written and carefully edited, but are among the best examples of "fine-press" work produced on the Pacific Coast.

Paul has now slowed down a bit in production, but still continues to turn out Westernlore volumes. Most of his works have been printed in small editions and were soon out of print, unattainable except at rare-book dealer's prices. Westernlore fortunately has lately seen fit to reprint some of these western gems, so perhaps they will be more available.

But in the field of the Death Valley '49ers, Inc., Paul has continued to remain active, serving first on the Advisory Board and later on the Board of Directors. He has been a great help to the Publication Committee in the publishing of the Keepsakes and their other booklets, and has served a number of times as chairman of the Author's Breakfast programs.

To those of us who have been so fortunate as to know Paul Bailey well, the trait that has probably endeared him the most has been his gentle and gracious manner and lively sense of humor. Talking to Paul and listening to Paul, as he tells of life as he has known it, is an unique experience. Paul has never been known to speak harshly of anyone, always drawing forth their best at any talkfest.

From such patriarchs of the Fortyniners as Ardis Walker, Burr Belden, Ed Ainsworth, John Hilton, Rodman Paul and Hollings C. Hollings, have come the legends incorporated in that charming chat he gave to us at the Fortyniners' 27th Annual Encampment, at the Author's Breakfast, held on the lawn of the golf course at Furnace Creek Ranch in November 1976, which he called, "An Unnatural History of Death Valley." These reflections on the "Valley's Varmints, Virgins, Vandals and Visionaries" — too choice to be forgotten—are preserved for posterity in this book.

*Sources include *POLOGAMY Was Better Than MONOTONY,* 1972, and *an ORAL HISTORY TAPE* of a talk with Paul Bailey, March 1978.

Traveling in style from Stovepipe Wells to Greenwater.

21

Going to the celebration in Death Valley in 1949. 20-mule team and attending wagons on their trek from Owens Valley to the Encampment.

BIGGEST

BIRTHDAY

BUST

AS ONE wanders around the bottommost reaches of Death Valley, observing with astonishment the annual encampment below sea level of the Death Valley '49ers—it is difficult to hide one's surprise and disbelief. Not only has the yearly '49er bash become the most lowdown party in America—but that unique barn-raising in the depths has become, unquestionably, America's greatest.

That Death Valley, in November, can attract up to 30,000 guests and wayfarers to a once-a-year birthday whingding—wearing everything—barbecue bibs, square dance bloomers, Stetsons and dogie pants—hard rock stretch jeans—carrying everything— kids, geetars, fiddles, cameras, paint brushes, typewriters, C-B radios, eight-track recorders, and jogging shoes. At last year's encampment, one visitor was observed walking the portico of Furnace Creek Inn—a dazed look on his face, a compass in one hand, and a computer calculator in the other.

And, on the road, it's sheer delight to watch them coming in to their lowdown party—riding everything, from painted vans to dune buggies, motorcycles to campers, jalopies to luxurious travel coaches, from four-wheel-drive Jeeps to motorized manure spreaders—not to mention horseback, muleback, and in rubber-tired Conestoga wagons. Were there such a thing as a twenty-mule-team left, you could be certain those archaic jackasses would somehow be pressed into service for this journey back to the promised

The First Death Valley Encampment on Saturday, December 3, 1949.

24

*The long line across the Valley floor. The Death Valley
Encampment of 1949, when up to 100,000 guests turned up for
the "Biggest Birthday Bust."*

land. If only for hugeness, oddity, and a strange sort of depravity in the depths—this annual campout has just got to be the most.

But for sheer size, magnitude, and strangeness, today's Death Valley birthday party becomes totally dwarfed by another one in this author's recollection.

To look backward from the same November date—to 1949—and one is shocked into recollection of what can only be termed the second Jayhawker Invasion—a penetration of such astonishing proportions that, unless you had not seen it, you could scarcely be expected to believe it. I can tell about it soberly and truthfully, because there are still a few trail-hardy souls showing up for the annual encampment who were in Death Valley on that fateful day so many years ago. I know, because I was in Death Valley all through that wild and incredible event.

In a far more important role—so was author and '49er director Ardis Manly Walker. It was Ardis Manly Walker who, instead of triumphantly leading this manswarm to safety on the valley floor, stood valiantly through a night and a day, with an armed posse, trying to halt the invasion — halt the vehicles — striving desperately to keep the spacious wastes of the Valley of Death from being inundated with humanity.

You see, 1949 was the centennial year of the discovery and dramatic penetration of this great natural wonder which, like Mecca, attracts so many pilgrims year after year. It had been 100 years since the Wades, the Briers, Jayhawkers, the Manly Party, and all the other heroic figures had written their tragedy and beauty into the historic sink to which they gave the name "Death Valley." It had been decided, on this hundredth anniversary, to stage a modest encampment, and invite a few thousand hardy souls to share a commemorative party in this land of weird and ghostlike history.

27

At a special Saturday luncheon, held at Ridgecrest, California, in November 1948, a group of delegates representing the counties of Inyo, San Bernardino, Los Angeles, and Kern, met, to ponder their respective community obligations in preparation for the coming Centennial observance for the State of California. Out of this meeting, and principally due to the urgings of Death Valley Monument Superintendent, T. R. Goodwin; and Paul Hubbard, Randsburg publisher, emerged a daring and harebrained decision—to stage their major centennial celebration in the forbidding and deathly depths of the valley!

To manage the affair, and to petition the state Centennial Commission for needed funds to underwrite it, the Death Valley '49ers organization was formed, and incorporated. Ardis Manly Walker and John Anson Ford are among the few stalwarts who remain of the original board members who promoted the affair. A. W. Noon was the '49ers first president; Maury L. Sorrells, was vice-president; John Anson Ford, secretary; and Arthur W. Walker was treasurer, with Joseph Micciche as his assistant, and also serving as secretary. The additional board members were George Baker, Charles A. Scholl, Otto K. Olson, Ardis Manly Walker, and Charles P. Salzer.

To tap the State Centennial Commission for funding of local observances, it was necessary that money be raised in the four counties adjoining Death Valley, to be matched dollar for dollar by the State. So the newborn Death Valley '49ers went energetically to work on the county boards of supervisors, corporations, and interested individuals. Their energetic solicitation brought quick and ample response.

With that taken care of, a bigger problem still remained. What kind of an observance and celebration would be most ap-

28

Governor of California would ride a multi-teamed stage coach.

propriate and appealing? Even with color and history for prece-
dence, it still seems totally weird that the '49ers would latch on
to the idea of a pageant as proper vehicle to mark Death Valley's
one hundred years—a pageant—in a forbidding wilderness. But
that was the decision.

In spite of the negatives, the Death Valley '49ers went stub-
bornly to work on what many considered an impossible dream.
Open predictions were made that they were certain to fall flat
on their desert jackasses. But, strangely, help came from many
sources. Dr. C. B. S. Evans cogitated on the past—and came up
with an heroic script for the drama. Later—when it turned out to
be a bit too garishly Hollywoodish, it was abandoned, rewritten,
and finally, with help from historian Frank Latta of Bakersfield,
was refined into the successful production it finally turned out to
be.

Then luck really walked in. Movie star James Stewart accepted the key post as narrator for the show. The eminent composer
Ferde Grofe offered to create special music for the event—including a special composition, "The Death Valley Suite," in majesty to
match his immortal "Grand Canyon Suite." The grand offer, how-
ever, was marred in the sequence of problems soon besetting the
event. Ferde Grofe became physically incapacitated before he could
complete his immortal score. He found it necessary to turn to the
music over to Frank Allan Hubbell for completion. Despite this
artistic setback, the "Death Valley Suite" still managed to emerge
as a classic. The whole project gained added emphasis when it was
announced that the orchestra backing up the pageant would be no
less than the renowned Hollywood Bowl Orchestra.

About this time, the '49er directors were truly worried about
their contract, which called for erection, in Desolation Canyon, of
grandstand facilities capable of seating 5,000 spectators. But with
true feel and rapport for the theme of this thing, and for the spec-
tacular forces they had set in motion, the Desolation Canyon
grandstands were erected, with materials transported hundreds of
miles over desert roads. And, in a supreme effort to counteract the

fear that already was permeating the organization — that not enough people would make the long haul into Death Valley to even partially fill the grandstands—additional talent was commandeered.

The Governor of California would ride a multi-teamed stagecoach in the pageant, to the crashing and exciting Grofe music, played by the Hollywood Bowl Orchestra. And, to give trained and polished voice, grace and glamor to the drama such Hollywood talent, besides James Stewart, the cast would include Gail Russell, Anne Revere, Guy Madison, Parley Baer, Charles Victor, Joseph Granby, M'Liss McClure, Kathleen Freeman, Chill Wills, Edgar Buchanan and Olive Mae Branch. Hundreds of other talented volunteers were added to the cast. It would be a pageant that would knock the bung-stoppers out of the water barrels!

The site for the pageant had been selected and chosen with thematic morbidity—Desolation Canyon—in the Valley of Death. To sort of lighten up this morguelike atmosphere, to help insure adequate attendance at an affair so bleakly promised, it was decided to add vocal backup to the Hollywood Bowl Orchestra. Get the combined glee clubs of the University of Redlands!

Magnificent and glamorous as were the plans and preparation, the publicity on the affair appeared to be increasingly negative. It was falling flat and ineffective on public ears. Great fears began to be felt by the '49ers that their coming show in Desolation Canyon would likely play to a desolate grandstand — a most desolate bust in vast and empty spaces.

So the hired publicity flacks were fired. Attempts were made by the directors to seed and plant a promotional garden in hopes of a rewarding and encouraging crop. Acting directly, they were even less effective. Finally, in desperation, the committee turned to that amazing '49er and author, Ed Ainsworth, of the *Los*

Angeles Times. A never-to-be-forgotten director of the '49er organization, a spellbinding speaker at many a later Death Valley author's breakfast and campfire, Ed Ainsworth was to win a peculiar and special immortality for what he accomplished for the Death Valley '49ers in 1949.

Gratuitously, and aided by the equally gracious and timely help of author Phil Townsend Hanna, of the Automobile Club of Southern California, Ed Ainsworth not only accomplished the impossible, but, with the skills and audacity of another Moses, he wrought the miracle of the Second Coming—complete with authentic wilderness, waste places, and on the floor of a Dead Sea.

A week before the big affair some of the more optimistic members of Death Valley '49ers allowed as how Ed Ainsworth's persuasive voice in the *Los Angeles Times,* and Phil Hanna's publicity pump at the Automobile Club might possibly bring as many as 15,000 visitors to Death Valley. Things indeed were looking up.

At this point I can only give it to you in the words of veteran director Ardis Manly Walker: "As the concluding days of preparation wore on it became apparent that all former guidelines must be tossed out the window. People were starting an earlier migration into Death Valley and in greater numbers than anyone had anticipated. At first this growing flood of traffic was hailed with a sense of relief by Lloyd Mitchell, Southern California manager for the California Centennials Commission, and Andy Noon, '49er president . . . They were glad of the assurance that enough people would be in attendance to make the investment worth-while.

"Then, as I took an after dinner walk out onto one of the terraces of Furnace Creek Inn on the eve of the pageant. I was greeted by a sea of campfires that covered the valley floor, and a stream of headlights extending along the highway as far north as the eye could see. At first glance this sight was reassuring to one who had been appointed by the '49ers to serve with Lloyd Mitchell as co-chairman of production. The scene brought a gulp to my throat and tears to my eyes. The people had responded . . ."

An understatement indeed. They had invaded Death Valley like a conquering army.

"In this moment of triumph," Ardis writes, "I ran my eyes along the pattern of traffic; bulging both lanes of the highway, cars moving four abreast, pushing the full blast of their headlights in one direction only—from north to south—directly into Desolation Canyon."

At that moment, triumph changed to consternation for Ardis. At last came realization that soon the canyon would be filled with the oncoming horde. Rehearsal was scheduled for early morning. The great pageant, in its entirety, must go on in the afternoon. In a matter of hours the canyon would be hopelessly clogged with automobiles and travel-weary pilgrims. There would be no room for tomorrow's show. There would be no possible chance for tomorrow's historical extravaganza.

Director Walker, grabbing up what sheriff's deputies and posse members were available, spent the remainder of the night erecting roadblocks; trying desperately to move the endless avalanche of cars in some other direction than the pageant site. Instead of 5,000 or 15,000 Californians showing up for the affair, the first '49ers Encampment was being literally swamped by impatient and weary visitors who had driven hundreds of miles, only to find themselves caught in a city-like traffic jam of monumental proportions.

Answering Ed Ainsworth's clarion call, the people had responded. Estimate of the number of jayhawkers participating in Death Valley's "second coming" runs from 60,000 to 125,000. Nobody really knows.

Stove Pipe Wells

35

A Clamper member in good standing is called a ''well jackass.''

36

THE CLAMPER CLAMPOUT

While all this was occurring, another invasion of '49ers, of strangely different type, had moved into Death Valley. They were encamped at Cow Mesa, on the historic ranch of Adolph Navares. This happened to be the ancient order of E Clampus Vitus, whose nefarious and tenuous roots go back to the earliest history of California—the gold rush days of 1849—some tireless E.C.V. researchers claim to have traced the order's lineage back to the Garden of Eden.

E Clampus Vitus membership is made up of California historians, and men of high and low repute—including some of the top brass of Death Valley '49ers, such as Ardis Walker, L. Burr Belden, Ronald Miller, Hugh Tolford, George Koenig, Sid Platford—you name them. The aims of E Clampus Vitus, of course, are altruistic and high: To mark and delineate the historic sites of California, and to take care of the widows and the orphans—particularly the widows.

A member in good standing is called a "well jackass." And their mysterious and peculiar conclaves are conducted under the light of the full moon. Under direction of such Noble Grand Humbugs as Carl Wheat, Roger Dalton, Eugene Biscailuz, Milford Springer, and Sid Platford, hundreds of these red-shirted, red-bearded Clampers were assembled on that moonlit night in 1949, at the creek and waterfall at Cow Mesa, 1400 feet above Desolation Canyon. They too had assembled to memorialize Death Valley's hundredth anniversary.

From the high and safe land shelf of Cow Mesa, the four hundred bloodshot eyes of two hundred loyal Knights of E Clampus Vitus were, that same night, looking down in consternation at what the hell was happening on Death Valley's floor. I know, because I was there. Sid Platford and other oldtime Humbugs and well jackasses of ECV know, because they too were there.

The affairs of E Clampus Vitus, luckily, didn't include the job of diverting 100,000 '49ers away from Desolation Canyon. But the next day, when it came time for this noble order to share in the big show at the grandstand site, they were just as totally traffic-jammed out of the spectacle as were the less fortunate campers caught at Wildrose Canyon.

Even Eugene Biscailuz, Sheriff of Los Angeles County, and Leo Carrillo, famous Spanish-American motion picture star, had to be back-packed from the Clamper Camp at Cow Mesa across the prickly valley floor, before they could mount their magnificent steeds and take their proper roles in the pageant. Other Knights of E Clampus Vitus, no matter how imperative the necessity, or how exalted the premise, were not so lucky in getting past the traffic jam. There were no helicopters in those days.

None of us who were present at the miraculous Second Coming in Death Valley, will ever forget it. And I can imagine there are other oldtimers and jayhawkers in Death Valley '49ers who have never forgotten it.

As you can see, there never really can be a natural history of Death Valley. The great pageant in Desolation Canyon was chronologically accurate—superbly produced and performed—enacted with taste and talent—probably the closest ever to come at natural history.

The real pageant of Death Valley—beginning in 1849—one hundred years earlier—and still marching by us—is really different. It seems to be a pageant that could have been sponsored by Hollywood—but wasn't. It's the most unnatural history imaginable. A parade of the damnedest weirdos—oddballs and freak-outs—ever to fly over the cuckoo's nest.

38

"Bishop" Paul Bailey, Judge, Burro Flapjack Race, 1958 Death
Valley '49er Encampment.

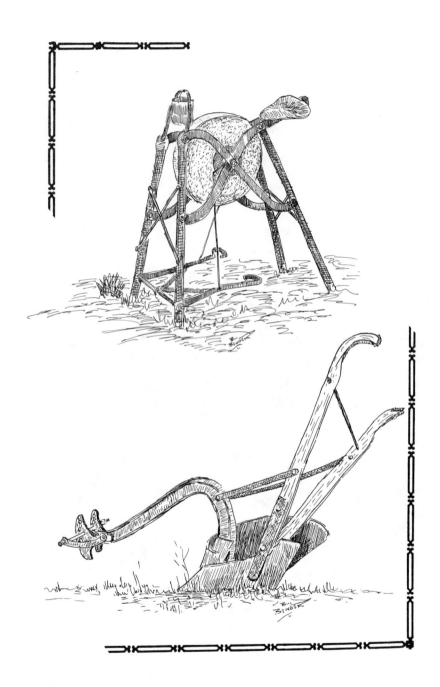

FARMER IN THE DELL

THE name Bennett comes constantly to mind in the lore of Death Valley—doubly so because there are two Bennetts—and both left enough legend and folklore behind them to render the pair an obtuse immortality. Asahel Bennett is the better known of the two because he was an important part of the original group who first entered Death Valley in 1849. His courageous and dogged battle with heat, thirst and starvation, as member of the Bennett-Arcane party, is amply attested and recorded.

It was Asahel Bennett who, realizing the Bennett-Arcane group was hopelessly stalled in Death Valley, sped William Lewis Manly and John Rogers over the mountains in search of help for his dying party. It was Asahel Bennett (after whom Bennett's Well is named), who shared the original campground at Furnace Creek. As one of the original '49ers he is rightly enshrined as a Death Valley hero. Asahel Bennett is likewise remembered as one of its heels.

Manly and Rogers, in their desperate journey, returned to Death Valley—bringing food and succor from Southern California to the Bennett-Arcane train left stranded in the desert wastes. Through the unselfish sacrifice of these young men, Asahel Bennett lived to reach civilization. At that point he sort of topples off his gilded chariot.

It was rumors of vast and neglected wealth that eventually lured Bennett back to Death Valley. It seems that a man by the name of Charles Alvord had lugged out some rocks that assayed high in gold. It was Bennett who guided Alvord back to the Valley of Death in hopes of rediscovering the spot where Alvord had picked up his gold-bearing rocks. When Alvord, in spite of Bennett's nagging and prodding, failed to come up with the answer, Bennett abandoned the poor wretch to the salt flats of Amargosa sink, to die of thirst and hunger.

Once more securely back in Los Angeles, Asahel Bennett accidentally ran into William Lewis Manly. He told Manly of his recent and aborted trip back to Death Valley; of the persistent amnesia of Charles Alvord as to location of his gold strike.

"We left that skunk back in the Valley," Bennett bragged.

Manly was horrified. "You abandoned him?"

"We abandoned him. He never told us where the gold was."

"Man, someone's got to rescue him! We must go back to the Valley!"

"Let the evasive rat die with his secret gold," Bennett argued.

But Manly remained adamant. Just because a man couldn't remember where in all of Death Valley he'd picked up a gold-bearing boulder was certainly not sufficient reason to sentence him to certain death. So, picking up an additional partner by the unlikely name of Caesar Twitchell, the three men once more braved the arid and lonely terrors of Death Valley in another search and rescue mission.

Eventually, after much hardship and suffering, they found Charles Alvord—stumbling around the lower valley reaches—mumbling to himself—still searching for the rocks with gold in them. But by the time the Bennett-Manly-Twitchell mission had located the lost Alvord, all supplies were used up. Now the four of them faced death from starvation, unless life's necessities were quickly procured.

So it was the brave and conscientious William Lewis Manly who agreed to stay on with the mumbling and searching Charles Alvord, while Asahel Bennett and Caesar Twitchell returned, with the pack mules, to Los Angeles, for the desperately needed help.

Neither of them ever returned to the suffering men, still bravely prospecting Death Valley. The point is, of course, that Asahel Bennett, the hero, turned out, in the end, to be Asahel the heel. It was bad enough for him to consign Charles Alvord to the grave. But for Bennett, the second time, to abandon his far more heroic fellow '49er, William Lewis Manly—along with the mumbling and groping Alvord—to die in the lethal wastes of the Valley of Death—smacks of dirty pool. Even though Manly did a repeat performance of his 1849 heroics, and climbed out again to safety—Bennett's actions were still anything but cricket.

But so much for Asahel Bennett. In our unnatural history, Asahel seems to come up more heel than hero.

A better candidate for any corkscrew chronicle, and certainly more in line with our type of protagonist, is the second Bennett— Bellerin' Teck Bennett.

What sets Bellerin' Teck Bennett apart is the fact that he had a pair of lungs with capacity and power to match his bull-like, querulous, and trumpeting voice. Even in ordinary conversation the voice of Bellerin' Teck ranged out in thunderous fortissimo. He'd never known what it was to whisper.

Legend declares that Bellerin' Teck Bennett landed in Death Valley in 1870—and probably because nobody could stand him, he came in alone. In the middle of nature's great cavity he stood—looking furtively around him at the miles of desert, rimmed with towering mountains. Here he found only abysmal and deathlike silence. Uneasy, and worried, he bellowed out like a bull with its tail in a gate-latch. When no answer or opposition greeted the vocal clamor, he looked about him once more at the immense spread of majestic scenery. Then, like a winging, possessive cock, he waved both his mighty arms outward and roared, "All this is mine!"

When not a sound of any voice answered to dispute or challenge him—when, instead of argument he received his answer in leagues of deathlike silence—he bellowed out again, "All this is mine, God damn it!"

His entire life, up to this moment, had been one continuous argument with humans who disputed and snarled back. More than anything he wanted some contentious man to shout out against him with "Like hell it's yours, Teck!" For, to Bellerin' Teck Bennett, to snort and argue was to live. But the nearest human this day was probably some desert Shoshone, at least fifty miles away. Not even Teck's mighty voice could carry that far.

Eventually Bellerin' Teck Bennett stopped yelling, looked around him, and what he saw was Furnace Creek, its bubbling springs, its refreshing spot of green in the wilderness. And what he saw looked good. Real good. Here old Loud-Mouth settled down, and here was started Furnace Creek Ranch. Only Bellerin' Teck did not call it Furnace Creek Ranch. To him, and to anyone within sound of his voice, it was "My Ranch."

He ran water from the springs and creek to his acres, and found that the desert soil was rich and responsive to irrigation. With the labor of his two hands he planted the little farm to

"All this is mine, God damn it," bellowed Bellerin' Teck Bennett.

"Mormon Jackson came into Death Valley with a wagon and two beautiful oxen."

barley and to alfalfa, and was amazed at their luxuriant growth. He soon had plenty of feed, but only undomesticated burros to enjoy it. And God never yet fashioned a desert jackass that would pull a plow. Teck is reputed to have brought the first quail into the Valley. They quickly found haven and peace in his green fields, and thrived abundantly. He had everything but farm animals to aid in the struggle. But without beasts to pull the plow, and truly aid him in the harvest, it was tedious and strenuous work for even his mighty muscles.

His solitary preservance at Furnace Creek lasted two years. And then entered the Mormon. The Mormon's name was Jackson—and he came into Death Valley with a wagon and two beautiful oxen. In line with his faith and convictions, Mormon Jackson had every intention of making the desert blossom like a rose. He hadn't counted on Bellerin' Teck Bennett.

What Bellerin' Teck gave Jackson was no gentle welcome. "By God, I own this!" came the bull-like trumpet. Teck swung his massive arms in arc-like gesture to indicate the whole valley. "It's mine! The whole thing!"

The Mormon stoically eyed the blustering farmer, and nodded at his precious oxen. "And, God be praised, I own both these beasts. They're mine—the pair of them!"

Bellerin' Teck eyed the oxen covetously. "Don't you try to squat here!" he roared. "Move on!" But Teck was mentally debating how he could gain possession of those beautiful oxen without surrendering any part of his domain.

At the same time the Lord had started revealing to the Mormon the truth of the mighty struggle going on in his adversary's mind. "All right, I shall move on. But that way, you'll never be able to use my oxen."

47

The two men, instead of standing facing one another, and shouting, began to circle warily—each intently eyeing the other. Finally Teck bellowed condescendingly. "Them *are* good lookin' animals!"

The Mormon looked about at the evidence of Teck's solitary husbandry. The earth indeed was blossoming. "And it looks like deep, rich soil here."

The inevitable happened. Bellerin' Teck caved in to reality. In the end, the two reputedly agreed to a partnership. "My Ranch" became a cooperative.

Unfortunately the partnership was too tenuous to last long. Quarrels were violent, bitter, and noisy. It is said the Bellerin' Teck eventually ran Mormon Jackson out at gunpoint—appropriating the oxen as earned rental for his intruder's stay in Death Valley.

But not even as tough a nut as Bellerin' Teck Bennett was able to endure many of the Valley's summers. Even he finally abandoned the original Furnace Creek Ranch—to be picked up later by wiser, less belligerent, and less noisy entrepreneurs.

Bellerin' Teck Bennett finally had to abandon his place.

The Marcy plan would have put a stop to marathon walks on the floor of Death Valley

THE MARCY PLAN

GIVE a little thought to the long ago. Go back to prehistoric times—and you'd probably find a ghostlike strangeness to Death Valley. And those of you who would prefer Death Valley ghostlike, strange and prehistoric—those of you who dislike it in its present state—a below sea-level, alkaline and mineralized sink of vast proportions—ought to take heart—to listen—to pay especial heed to what Engineer E. L. Marcy has in mind for it. Definitely you should alert yourselves as to what he hopes to do about it.

The Marcy plan, in its published thesis, is simply a novel and practical idea to reverse history. In essence, it will restore Death Valley to its original pristine beauty—a placid sea of fresh water extending the length of the big dish, and well over '49ers' heads at most points.

Once the Marcy restoration is accomplished, the Amargosa River will again flow southward—willowed—teeming with fish and wild fowl—a meandering stream of especial beauty and appeal. Death Valley's future great lake will be a paradise for fishing, boating, and water skiing—a source of moisture not only to the timbered hills and canyons surrounding it, but will change the entire climate for hundreds of square miles—from summer's hot hell to the living green of forests and meadows.

The amazing rejuvenation of this great waste place, as proposed and blueprinted by Mr. Marcy, is so simple that one cannot understand why it has not long ago been put into operation. Had that been so, Death Valley's annual authors' breakfasts, and artists' breakfasts, and even the fiddlers' contests, could very well have been enjoyed from the passenger deck of such Death Valley steamboats as *The Furnace Queen* or *The Stovepipe Queen* as they cruised toward Wingate Inlet.

51

How is such a wonder to be accomplished? Very simply. All that is necessary, in the Marcy Plan, is for the city of Los Angeles to put a syringe clamp on its sewer lines before they can empty themselves futilely and uselessly into the Pacific Ocean. Send this precious, life-giving ecological tide flowing the other direction! Where? Into the Valley of Death!

Since sewage—even Los Angeles sewage—is more than 90% water—and since this water is tapped in immeasurable quantities from the Feather River, the Owen's River, the Colorado River, and hundreds of wells—only to be flushed down the johns and sinks of a million homes and sent out to sea—where there already is enough water—I cannot believe but what Engineer Marcy is ecologically and brilliantly on target. A neat and practical idea like that cannot long go unfulfilled.

And how does he plan to reverse the flow of life-giving sewage from the Pacific outfall into this thirsty Valley? Simply by boring a tunnel, at sea level, in direct line, under the San Gabriel Mountains, a portion of the Mojave Desert, aimed directly at Owl Lake sink, and out into Death Valley through the Owlshead Mountains—a bit southerly—so as to narrowly avoid flooding Wingate Pass.

Don't worry about the gook and the gunk that might come in with the john water. Marcy convincingly proves that Nature long ago provided, in the right chemical balance, and in the right place, the ingredients and emoluments to miraculously and swiftly purify this live-giving moisture in its endless and limitless quantities. The chemicals which once purified the waters of that great lake which, in prehistoric times lay far above the level of Furnace Creek's new high-rises—now lies waiting and eager on this dry sink and lake-bed to go instantly to work on the worst that Los Angeles can send us. Result? Pure, potable H_2O. Fish, trees, grass, orchards, boating, water-skiing, and the chance for present Death Valley '49ers to conduct an authors' breakfast, an artists' break-

The Stovepipe Queen

Mr. Marcy's Artesian Well.

fast, or a fiddlers' contest from the passenger deck of a cruising steamboat.

But I, for one, do not rate the Marcy Plan for the rejuvenation of Death Valley as facetious or far-fetched. I am of the opinion that anything once imagined, eventually becomes a reality.

If we can talk to and photographically view the planet Mars, even chemically analyze its soil, 250 million miles away—if we can dispatch a squad of our own citizens to walk around and prospect for rocks on the moon—rest assured that the wetting down of Death Valley with Los Angeles john water is not only possible, but very probable.

But the certainty and probabilities of the Marcy Plan *do* make me feel a bit uneasy. Something naggingly whispers that, if all of us live long enough, we *can* and *will* boat up the Amargosa. The only consolation—other than the climatic and aquatic switch—is that it will be a hell of a lot easier to cruise the Valley than to hike it, jeep it, or ride camels around it, as some earlier nuts thought so neat. Or—as some hyperactive jugheads now do it—by jogging across its dry bottom, in the heat of summer.

THE FAMILY PLAN

BECAUSE some like it hot—some like it dry—and some like the seclusion which distance gives—it is no mystery why Death Valley and its surrounding desert and mountains, has become an increasingly popular rendezvous and retreat to families. Here, in this vast and hidden wilderness, families can relax, cavort, and do their things in freedom, and without restraint.

Many famous families, for years, have made Death Valley their hideaway from the hustle and bustle of city pressure. And certainly no family whoever found this vast area suitable to their collective wants, was more famous than the Manson Family. Charles Manson, probably the most widely known family-head and Big Daddy-O, is quoted as saying: "This place has got everything."

Years before Death Valley Basin became a National Monument, much of its area was cut up into ranch sites—interleaved with mining claims. Furnace Creek Ranch, as we have already observed, was once a bonafide ranch site—as was the Navares Ranch at Cow Springs, on the hills overlooking the Valley floor—and the Barker Ranch to the southeast.

It was the old Barker Ranch which especially appealed to Charlie Manson. Not only was it an ideal place where he and his family could rest and recuperate from the killing pace of the city, but offered more seclusion and better facilities than did the Spahn Ranch, which his family had already made famous.

This place, at the lower end of Death Valley, seemed absolute fulfillment to Biblical prophecy. You see, Charles Manson, in addition to his other accomplishments, was an especially apt and sharp Bible scholar. He was also a soul-fired musician—with leanings toward the chorded far out. He had pored over the scriptures until he'd become totally obsessed—and a little confused. Was he Lucifer? Or was he Jesus Christ incarnate? He seemed to be a trifle more inclined toward the latter idea. As Jesus, it seemed to be the proper and appropriate thing for him and his loyal family to initiate the great Second Coming, as predicted in the Book of Revelation. And it was especially impressive to think that one had only to reverse the syllables of Man-Son, and it became the Son of Man.

For spiritual guidance in their Death Valley sojourn, the Manson Family developed a dynamic liturgy, choosing as guiding creed the twin admonitions of Revelation 9, from the Bible—and "Revolution 9," from the Beatles' recordings and soundtrack.

"And he opened the bottomless pit; and there arose a smoke out of the pit . . . and there came out of the smoke locusts upon the earth . . . and unto them was given power, as the scorpions of the earth have power . . . and the shapes of the locusts were like unto horses prepared unto battle; and on their heads were as it were crowns like gold, and their faces were as the faces of men.

"And they had hair as the hair of women . . . and they had breastsplates of iron; and the sound of their wings was as the sound of chariots of many horses running to battle . . .

"And they had a king over them, which is the angel of the bottomless pit . . ."

The Beatles song and music of "Revolution 9" was one hell of a lot more wild and gibberish than Revelation 9, from the Bible—but it too had its inflammatory and rallying cry. The Manson Family locust-chariots were, of course, the dune buggies they

Barker Ranch

"This place has got everything."

had appropriated, brought into Barker flats, shielded with biblical breastplates of iron, armed with machine guns, and propelled with many horses.

When the Manson Family arrived in Death Valley, their grunt-headed messiah, by a series of avenging angel tactics in Los Angeles, had already considered he'd started the titanic struggle that would wipe out mankind on earth. Diabolical human butchery, with the racially pitched notes and mementoes left behind, had been the Family's plan—the blacks would be blamed, and the white reprisal would touch off the mighty black-white holocaust— the bloody cataclysm predicted in Revelation. So sure was Charlie Manson that he'd gotten Revelation 9 and "Revolution 9" moving, he ordered Paul Watkins, family accomplice, to explore with scuba equipment, the depths of Death Valley's "Devil's Hole." Here, far down in the "bottomless pit," he had hopes there might be standing or sitting room where the Family could safely take time out from the war they had started, as it inevitably moved on to consume the world.

Manson's "Second Coming," of course, would be accomplished with frightening power. War games, with his armed and plated dune buggies, preparatory to the locusts swarming in on the establishment and destroying the world, were on in full force at Barker Ranch—when the law finally stepped in and put stop to the family fun.

Since the Manson Family were ejected from Death Valley as flagrant violators of the rules, it is now permissive again, and quite proper, for families to again enjoy Death Valley. Park Service officials, of course, are hopeful family visitors will be less rough and roisterous. It's all right for you to have your fun in the sun— but management would prefer you didn't get carried away with

61

it. Dune buggies are strictly forbidden—no matter how few or how many horses. And so are machine guns.

Death Valley has often been considered the bottomless pit. By those who have dug deep for riches. By the Manson Family, who were going to unleash from it the biblical locusts of destruction upon the world. And from the engineers who still hope to resurrect it as an alpine like by channeling in the Los Angeles sewer line. But, thank God, up to now, it's somehow been saved from all of them.

Greenwater Ranch became Furnace Creek Ranch.

GREENWATER, GREENWATER —

WHERE HAVE YOU GONE?

DEATH VALLEY, with its picturesque outback, has almost universally become the picture of a romanticized spot—sparked first by tragic happenings—rediscovered by idealistically-minded nature lovers—and now publicized into the world's most desirable vacation place.

It is America's great sub-sea-level salton sink. A geologic paradise. A study of ages past. To others, including many of the modern '49ers, it is the place where ghosts walk. It doesn't matter that one can sense and enjoy their ghostly presence even while luxuriating over a Fred Harvey breakfast, served at Furnace Creek, on a green and palm-studded golf course.

If you have wondered if my words are purposely meant to disturb the accepted image of a silent and sublime spot for a winter vacation—you are right. Death Valley's ghosts are still present, all right—ghosts of some of the damnedest, weirdist towns and cities ever spawned.

The first citizens of Death Valley—excluding the Indians, who enjoyed this place a long time before '49ers discovered it— were pioneers of great courage and heroic stature. But among the later habituees of Death Valley and its immediate suburbs were some freaks more colorful and unbelievable than anything in Barnum's museum.

Are you aware that just east of Dante's View was the city of Greenwater? That Greenwater was touted as "the greatest copper camp on earth?" Although Greenwater totally lacked water, and was anything but green, its ebullient city fathers promised that within two years its mines would produce a hundred times the ore coming from the rich digs of Butte, Montana and Bingham, Utah. Underlying Greenwater, it was claimed, was an area twelve miles long and five miles wide, composed 75% of pure copper.

So Greenwater unblushingly declared itself to be the greatest copper discovery since Lake Superior, divided itself into mining

claims, and peddled the claims for a total of $4,000,000 to a frenzied herd of promoters. And suddenly here was a city blossomed over a reputed big bonanza. A city made up of the strangest assortment of stock swindlers ever assembled in one place.

Before a single mine could prove itself, Greenwater's copper stock was listed on the New York Stock Exchange. Tycoons T. L. Oldie, W. A. Clark, Charles M. Schwab, and others, promptly subscribed $25,000,000 to the Greenwater Copper Mine & Smelter Company. To serve a suddenly burgeoning community, a $100,000 bank was established in a sheet iron building, along with two of Death Valley's most colorful newspapers—one of them the *Death Valley Chuck-Walla.*

It seems unbelievable in retrospect that not one of Greenwater's glory holes ever produced enough copper to pay the cost of the water haul. But the crooks, the gamblers, the drunks, the earth scratchers, the saloons, the whores, and the Greenwater freaks, lived on in well adjusted community life until the "greatest copper camp on earth" literally dissolved and disintegrated under the sun.

The girls who serviced Greenwater were an especially hardy breed. Sawtooth Annie is reputed to have papered the inside of her tenthouse with the copper certificates she'd accepted in payment for tricks through a long and useful life. Certainly Annie rates as a stellar example of civic loyalty and pride.

"Hooch Simpson"

PANIC AT PANAMINT

THE SKIDS TO SKIDOO

NOT all of Death Valley's vanished satellite cities squatted over barren holes. Panamint City and "23 Skidoo" perched themselves in the barren mountains of the west rim. But those barren hills proved anything but barren of silver. Had the silver ore held out as promised, Furnace Creek would probably have turned out to be another industrial metropolis instead of a center for dreaming and relaxation. And there would be a lot less ghost town nostalgia purveyed out of our lowdown Valley.

Panamint City, most promising of the two, was born in 1873—produced, prospered, and perished. But not before spawning its share of desert freak-outs. All that's left now of Panamint City is the chimney of its brewery—a very fitting monument— and the record of its turbulent days, including the testimony of some of the strange characters who inhabited it. '49er director and author, George Koenig, has written touchingly of Skidoo and Panamint City. His chronicle of their life and times is a Death Valley '49er publication.

Over the years the liars and the hopefuls have tried to revive Panamint City. To no avail. Only the ghosts remain, and what they said about it.

> Panamint, Panamint, city of gold
> Where the women were crazy, sweaty and bold,
> And the likker would pizen a sidewinder's hole,
> One year at Panamint made any man old.

Skidoo was of later vintage—also perched high on the Panamints—and claiming to have that rarest of novelties in Death

Valley—drinking water. This potable liquid was brought over a 23 mile pipeline from Telescope Peak, and could have influenced the town's nonsensical name—"23 Skidoo"—from the popular and "in" saying of that day— equally nonsensical—meaning, "get the hell out."

"Controversy also prevails as to Skidoo's parentage," says George Koenig. Some tout a John Ramsey and his partner, 'One Eye' Thompson. Some credit Harry Ramsey, Art Holliday and Frank Flynn. Others give the honor to Steve Hovic, as well as Bob Montgomery of Rhyolite fame. You 'place your bets and takes your chances.' You have little to lose; for the men, the mines, the town are gone, leaving one opinion as good as another."

Taken singly or collectively, the reputed fathers of Skidoo were a gaggle of kooks, and their town a kooky one indeed.

Skidoo was over 5600 feet high—nestled between Tucki Mountain and Emigrant Pass—possessed a telegraph line to the outer world—a 23-mile water pipeline—a postoffice, three restaurants, two boarding houses, seven saloons. It possessed also Joe Simpson—the only man who was ever hanged twice.

According to an eye-witness report in the *Skidoo News:* "The comparative quiet of Sunday morning was broken by a wild disturbance that resulted in the brutal murder of James Arnold, one of Skidoo's most prominent citizens, inasmuch as he had located the townsite. It ended in the lynching of his assailant, Joe Simpson, a local saloonkeeper and gun-fighter.

"Simpson, locally known as 'Hooch' owing to his fondness for the liquor known by that name, had been indulging . . . and was in a highly inflamed state. Joe was also without funds, a condition not calculated to improve his usual bad temper, and to his disordered imagination the only practical way of getting it was to hold up a bank.

"For this purpose he entered the Skidoo Trading Company's store, in which the Southern California Bank is located. He immediately covered the cashier, Ralph E. Dobbs, with his gun, and demanded twenty dollars under penalty of instant death . . ."

That's what is known in the wild west as a "sight draft."

"A wild rush ensued and before he could carry out his threats he was overpowered. He became so abusive to everyone that Jim Arnold, the manager, eventually put him out of the store by force."

Apparently this sort of bugged Hooch Simpson, who resented being tossed out by Jim Arnold. So he rearmed himself, went back to the bank section of the store. He strode directly to the bank counter, and again accosted Arnold:

"Have you got anything against me, Jim?"

"No, Joe, I've got nothing against you," Arnold genially replied.

"Yes you have. Your end has come. Prepare to die!"

And so Joe Simpson, a sourdough sorehead if there ever was one, and apparently lacking any sense of humor, proceeded to shoot banker Jim Arnold in the heart.

After an inquest over Arnold's corpse, an armed body of citizenry snatched Hooch Simpson from sheriff's custody, and hanged him to a telegraph pole. But, after they had taken the culprit's body down, and the telegraph wires had sped the news of the lynching to the outer world, Skidoo was soon overwhelmed by a rush of newspaper reporters from other parts of California.

73

Joe Simpson who was hanged twice to oblige visiting journalists. Skidoo justice and hospitality at its best.

Skidoo mill.

The white buildings in Skidoo were typical of cities that sprang up overnight built by covering the frames with white tenting.

They brought with them their best photographers to record the strange happenings at Skidoo.

Imagine their disappointment to find, on arrival, that Simpson no longer was dangling from a telegraph pole. But in a rare gesture of municipal cooperation and goodwill, the citizenry of Skidoo rose to the occasion. Realizing that the photographers had made a long, dry trip, with little to show for it, they obligingly reenacted the hanging, by again stringing Simpson up, so that suitable and newsworthy photos could be taken.

Aside from the fact that a case could be argued for "double jeopardy," and that poor Hooch had paid twice for his crime, he apparently made no protest. Worse, after reburial, Hooch was obligingly dug up a second time in order to accommodate a visiting physician in need of an office skull. Hooch went the third time down—minus his head.

According to Death Valley logic, the moral reads: "Don't get hung up over a sight draft, and, if possible, do try to keep your head."

If Skidoo's parlor houses were ever counted, it remains a secret to history. Again only the crazy ghosts report:

> There was a cat house in Skidoo,
> That was perched on a peak for the view,
> But the miners who climbed it,
> Seemed never to mind it,
> For the girls always knew what to do.

Author George Koenig charmingly tells of "Blonde Betty," one of Skidoo's sporting ladies who apparently knew exactly what to do. "It's one of Shorty Harris' stories," George explains, "which means it just might have been stretched a bit.

"It seems that 'Skagway' Thompson, 'as fine a chap as ever drew a cork,' passed away. Touched by the sight of the shady ladies from Skidoo's red light row, the only women in camp at that time, strewing wildflowers about the grave, Shorty Harris talked to the traveling preacher who was in town and agreeable to saying a few words at the graveside. It was also decided to have someone sing 'Skagway's' favorite song. 'Blonde Betty' was selected. In describing her lark-like voice to the preacher, it was deemed best to omit that she was one of the camp's 'fallen sparrows.'

"According to Shorty, Blonde Betty was as pretty as a curly ribbon, and with the preacher being young and good looking the lass was hustled away as soon as the services were over, lest her sweetly lilting notes be soured by an unfortunate revelation.

"But that next day? Well, it's Shorty's story, so let's listen to him: '. . . I saw her and the Parson picking wildflowers. Of course he didn't know then what she was. After that I reckon he didn't care. He chucked the preaching job and ran off with Betty. But maybe God went along. They got married and live over in Nevada, and you couldn't find a happier family or a finer brood of children anywhere.' "

Scotty's Castle.

BIRDS OF PASSAGE

TO A writer attempting to do anything on the natural history of Death Valley—it always comes out the most unnatural history imaginable. In this, of course, one must totally exclude such sober works as those pertaining to its heroic past, its geology, its economic contribution to America's mineral wealth.

But history, in its nitty gritty, must of necessity hone in on people. And I swear that the people who brought life and animation to Death Valley, were the damnedest assortment of kooks, characters and bullshitters ever turned loose on a dry and ancient lake bed.

As oddballs and unmitigated liars, where could one ever top such a pair as Shorty Harris and Death Valley Scotty? They left us a legacy of such color and lunacy as to defy comparison. For Shorty, a string of ghost towns, glory holes, and tall tales that will titillate generations unborn. From Death Valley Scotty—"the fastest con man in the west"—the Castle, the Battle of Wingate Pass, and a line of crap about secret gold mines so brilliantly concocted and so masterfully told that all of us—including myself—still believe it.

Take
>That old desert rat from Zabriskie,
>And his jackass, especially friskie,
>>Claimed every rock from his mine,
>>Came out gold every time.
>Why? Because he dipped horny toads
>>In his whiskey.

Death Valley characters: Shorty Harris and Seldom Seen Slim.

Death Valley Scotty portrait painted by Orpha Klinker.

"Wild history definitely is made by wild people."

One can speak endlessly on the freakiness of things pertaining to Death Valley—from ghost towns, sewage resurrection, to armored dune buggies, and camel caravans—and never come near to exhausting the subject, or scraping out the basin. There just is not room to adequately detail and explain the scores and scores of strangely-motivated humans who have wandered this lowdown Valley.

Maybe it's the heat. Maybe it's the low altitude. Maybe it's the gold corybantics. Maybe it's the borax syndrome. Certainly something attracts oddballs to this place, as surely as a sugar-boil attracts flies. All I know is that some of the most outlandish, improbable, and interesting people on earth found refuge, comfort and freedom in Death Valley.

So, to the kooks of the world—welcome! It's Home, Sweet Home! Wild history definitely is made by wild people.

The natural history of Death Valley just ain't natural. It has its own way of flowering out of weird and wonderful characters.

Death Valley's people are never dull or normal. It's a strange bottom of the world to sit in. Strange people enjoy sitting there. And, since today's crop of '49ers seem to inexplicably dote on the unnatural attraction of this place — maybe they too are a bit mentally out of phase.

But isn't it wonderful to be crazy? In this crazy place?

The Death Valley prospectors best friends and helpers.